T0169870

Boiled Sweets & Hard Candy

Boiled Sweets & Hard Candy

20 traditional recipes for home-made chews, taffies, fondants & lollipops

Claire Ptak

LORENZ BOOKS

This edition is published by
Lorenz Books, an imprint of
Anness Publishing Ltd,
Blaby Road, Wigston,
Leicestershire LE18 4SE

info@anness.com

www.lorenzbooks.com;
www.annesspublishing.com

If you like the images in this book
and would like to investigate using
them for publishing, promotions or
advertising, please visit our website
www.practicalpictures.com for
more information.

© Anness Publishing Ltd 2013

Publisher: Joanna Lorenz
Editor: Kate Eddison
Photographer: Nicki Dowey
Food Stylist: Claire Ptak
Food Stylist's Assistants: Kate
   McCullough and Adriana Nascimento
Prop Stylists: Wei Tang and
   Marianne de Vries
Designer: Lisa Tai
Production Controller: Pirong Wang

PUBLISHER'S NOTE

Although the advice and information in this book are believed to be accurate and
true at the time of going to press, neither the authors nor the publisher can accept
any legal responsibility or liability for any errors or omissions that may have been
made nor for any inaccuracies nor for any loss, harm or injury that comes about
from following instructions or advice in this book.

NOTES

- Bracketed terms are intended for American readers.
- For all recipes, quantities are given in both metric and imperial measures and,
  where appropriate, in standard cups and spoons. Follow one set of measures,
  but not a mixture, because they are not interchangeable.
- Standard spoon and cup measures are level. 1 tsp = 5ml, 1 tbsp = 15ml,
  1 cup = 250ml/8fl oz.
- Australian standard tablespoons are 20ml. Australian readers should use 3 tsp in
  place of 1 tbsp for measuring small quantities.
- American pints are 16fl oz/2 cups. American readers should use 20fl oz/2.5 cups
  in place of 1 pint when measuring liquids.
- Electric oven temperatures in this book are for conventional ovens. When using a fan
  oven, the temperature will probably need to be reduced by about 10–20°C/20–40°F.
  Since ovens vary, you should check with your manufacturer's instruction book
  for guidance.
- The nutritional analysis given for each recipe is calculated for the total quantity.
  The analysis does not include optional ingredients.
- Medium (US large) eggs are used unless otherwise stated.

Front cover image shows Lemon Drops, for recipe see page 22.

Contents

Introduction
6

Working with Sugar
8

Hard Candies and Lollipops
20

Chews and Fondants
48

Introduction

Everyone has their favourite boiled sweet, hard candy or pulled taffy, and whether you suck them slowly or crunch them up, they are always satisfying. Made with sugar syrup and a variety of other ingredients, they require a little effort to make, but the results are well worth it. Fondants are made using a slightly different process, giving them a softer texture.

Sugar

The very foundation stone of confectionery is sugar. Fancy sugar-work goes back centuries, and we have proof that spun sugar threads were made into nests and dishes to decorate banqueting tables in China at least 500 years ago. If sugar is cooked at a high

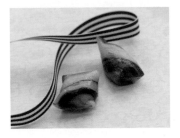
Above: Traditional Peppermint Humbugs.

temperature, it begins to caramelize. This caramelized sugar can be spun into beautiful lacy shapes by drizzling it, when melted, over something such as a wooden spoon handle or rolling pin to shape it. Or it can be drizzled directly on to a confection to decorate it.

More intricate sugar work is done by transforming a cooled, pliable mass of sugar syrup into shapes (such as candy canes or

aniseed twists) by stretching and pulling. Master confectioners can even blow bubbles in the mixture and make delicate, elaborate shapes from the sugar that resemble glass figures. A sugar syrup is quite simply sugar that is dissolved in water and then heated. From the resultant solution, these

Above: Old-fashioned Pear Drops can be shaped in classic moulds.

Above: Worked sugar can be shaped and coloured in endless ways.

two simple ingredients can form the basis of many things, from chewy taffies and soft fondant to boiled sweets and lollipops.

The proportion of sugar to water is a factor in the finished product, but the result has more to do with how much water is boiled away in the cooking process. During cooking, the syrup reaches various stages, from a delicate translucent thread to a dark and rich caramel.

Creating different confections

The simplest hard-boiled sweets and candies are made from a sugar syrup heated to the hard-crack stage, then allowed to set in shapes. Beautiful moulds are available in traditional designs, which give delightful results. Alternatively, the sugar syrup can be heated to the soft-crack stage, then manipulated by pulling and stretching. This process incorporates hundreds of tiny air bubbles into it, lightening the colour and texture. The length of time the syrup is worked will dictate

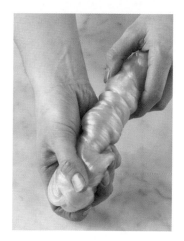

Above: Sugar syrups are stretched and pulled to create different textures.

the finished result – whether hard and glossy or soft and chalky. Chewy taffies, such as salt-water taffy, are brought only to the hard-ball temperature, which creates a soft finish. The softest type of confection in this book, fondant, is brought to an even lower temperature – the soft-ball stage – and then worked with the hands until it forms a smooth sugarpaste.

Right: Lollipops are a favourite for children all around the world.

Using this book

The introductory section of this book covers all the basics you will need to know before you embark on your sweet-making adventure. The chart on pages 14–15 illustrates the different stages of sugar syrups, and it's a good idea to familiarise yourself with this before you begin. A handy guide to tools and equipment is included, so grab your sugar thermometer and start making your own delicious confectionery!

Working with Sugar

Sweet- and candy-making requires you to have a couple of items of special equipment and to learn a few techniques before you begin. Sugar syrups are very delicate and they have to be handled in a certain way. The following pages will guide you through the process, with step-by-step instructions for making a sugar syrup, pulling taffy and making fondant, as well as a guide to recognizing all the stages of heating a sugar syrup.

Sugar-working Equipment

It is an undeniable fact that a few essential pieces of cooking equipment will make sweet- and candy-making at home much easier and more rewarding. Keen cooks will have most of these items in the kitchen already, and may only need to invest in a couple of extra utensils, such as a copper pan and a sugar thermometer, to get started.

A good quality, unlined, solid copper pan with a heavy base is always worth the money. There is no better container in which to boil sugar. The copper conducts heat more efficiently than other metals, and also looks most attractive hanging in the kitchen.

Use wooden spatulas or wooden spoons for stirring hot syrup and nut brittle, as they will not conduct the heat to your hand or melt in the mixture. A wooden spatula is also useful for working fondant to a light texture.

A marble slab is essential for sweet-makers, as it forms a perfect surface on which to work sugar syrups.

Below: Marble slab.

Above: Baking parchment.

There are several different kinds of baking paper available. Waxed and greaseproof paper are best used as a wrapper for finished sweets. Baking parchment is usually the most appropriate for oven use; silicone paper is

Above: Copper pan.

Below: Funnel and metal scraper

more expensive and even more non-stick than parchment. There are also reusable liners on the market. These should be kept flat or rolled; to clean them, wash gently with warm soapy water and dry well.

The most important tool in sweet-making, at the heart of many of the recipes in this book, is a sugar thermometer. It should be clearly marked with the temperature in Celsius and/or Fahrenheit, plus

Left: Sugar thermometer.

the main stages for sweet-making, for example 'thread', 'soft-ball', 'firm-ball' and 'hard-ball'. Sugar thermometers are very fragile and should be wrapped for storage. Glass and plastic measuring jugs (cups) for liquid are essential, while sturdy metal, ceramic or plastic measuring spoons are vital for adding small quantities of ingredients.

A funnel with a catch mechanism is another wonderfully useful pouring tool that allows a specific amount of liquid to be measured out.

A metal scraper is essential for working sugar syrups into fondants and taffies – you will need one for most of the recipes in this book.

Thin metal spatulas are ideal for lifting confections from baking sheets or coaxing sweets out of moulds. You can buy reusable metal moulds for your confections, including some very pretty antique-style types.

A pair of kitchen scissors can be used to cut sweets, such as Lemon Drops, into shape.

Finally, digital scales are a must for the sweet-maker's kitchen. They give very accurate readings and will ensure absolute precision when measuring the tiny quantities that are required of certain ingredients in these recipes.

Above: Antique sweet mould.

Making a Sugar Syrup

Many of the sweets in this book begin life as a basic sugar syrup. A sugar syrup is quite simply sugar that is dissolved in water and then heated. From the resultant solution, these two simple ingredients can form the basis of myriad things, from chewy taffies and soft fondant to boiled sweets and hard candies.

How to make a sugar syrup

To make a simple sugar syrup you will need a clean, dry, heavy pan that is large enough to accommodate three to four times the volume of ingredients. Using an unlined copper pan will always yield the best results, but you can use a large, heavy stainless-steel pan instead. Read through the recipe and get all the ingredients and equipment needed together before you start. You need to keep a close eye on sugar syrup, so you cannot leave the kitchen or start preparing something else while it is cooking. Prepare an ice-water bath and set it aside. You will also need a long-handled wooden spoon, a sugar thermometer and a clean pastry brush to hand.

Using and Checking Your Sugar Thermometer

• Before making your syrup, you should check the accuracy of your thermometer by placing it in a pan of water and bringing the water to a boil. Water boils at 100°C/212°F. If the temperature on your thermometer varies from this, be sure to make the same adjustment when preparing your sugar syrup.

• Sugar thermometers are very delicate pieces of equipment, and should be stored and used carefully. A sugar thermometer can crack if it is immersed into boiling temperatures straight from cold. To avoid this, always let it sit in in a jug or pitcher of hot water before immersing it in a boiling sugar syrup.

1 Place the amount of sugar specified in the recipe in the pan. If the recipe calls for any additional ingredient to sugar and water, add that to the sugar at this stage. Add the quantity of water specified in the recipe to the pan. Using a long-handled wooden spoon (which will withstand the heat better than a metal or plastic spoon), slowly stir the sugar and water together over a moderate heat, until the sugar has dissolved.

2 Insert a sugar thermometer and bring the syrup to a boil. Do not let the thermometer touch the bottom or sides of the pan, as this will affect the temperature reading. Most sugar thermometers come with a clip that can be attached to the side of the pan, suspending it in the syrup. Do not stir the mixture at this stage. If any small crystals have formed along the edge of the pan at this stage, they can be gently coaxed back into the sugar syrup with a clean, dampened pastry brush.

3 Let the mixture continue to cook until it reaches the desired stage and temperature as described in the recipe. If you do not have a sugar thermometer, you can test the stage of your syrup in a bowl of cold water instead (using the chart on pages 14–15), but using a thermometer and the cold-water test together will give the most accurate and reliable results. When it has reached the temperature, stop the cooking by dipping the base of the pan into the ice-water bath.

Testing for a Set

Many of the recipes in this book will require you to bring the sugar syrup to a certain stage. A sugar thermometer has the names of these stages, along with the temperatures, marked on. However, you can also test to see if you have achieved a stage by using the cold water test. This is called 'testing for a set'.

To test for the set indicated in the recipe, drop a teaspoonful of the sugar syrup into a cup of very cold water and test as indicated below. This chart is best used in conjunction with a sugar thermometer, to ensure you achieve the most accurate results. Keep a close eye on the sugar thermometer as the syrup is heating and test it as soon as it is getting close – do not heat the syrup too much, as once you have passed the required stage, you cannot take it back.

	Stage	Temperature	Cooking instructions	Ideal for:
	THREAD	106–112°C; 223–234°F	Lift the sugar solution lightly from the water with your fingers or a spoon – it should form a short thread. If not, continue cooking it until the syrup is a few degrees hotter.	A binding agent for nut pastes.
	SOFT-BALL	112–116°C; 234–240°F	While the syrup is still submerged in the water, form it into a small ball with your fingers. Remove the ball from the water – if it feels sticky, loses its shape and flattens out, it is at the soft-ball stage.	Turkish delight, marzipan, fudge and fondant.

	Stage	Temperature	Cooking instructions	Ideal for
	FIRM-BALL	118–120°C; 244–240°F	While the syrup is still submerged in the water, form it into a small ball. Remove the ball from the water and hold it between your fingers. It should feel sticky, but hold its shape while still being malleable.	Caramel and divinity.
	HARD-BALL	121–130°C; 250–266°F	While the syrup is still submerged in the water, it should easily form into a ball. Remove the ball from the water and hold it between your fingers. If it is sticky, but holds its shape and is rather rigid, it is at the hard-ball stage.	Marshmallows and salt-water taffy.
	SOFT-CRACK	132–143°C; 270–290°F	Remove the syrup from the water and stretch it between your fingers – it should be slightly sticky and form a brittle thread that is bendable at first, but then cracks.	Taffy, toffee and Edinburgh rock.
	HARD-CRACK	149–154°C; 300–310°F	Remove the solidified syrup from the water. It should no longer feel sticky and will break easily. It should also have a slightly yellow colour.	Barley sugar, lollipops and spun sugar.

Working with Fondant

The name 'fondant' comes from the French word fondre, which means 'to melt'. It is a smooth, rich, opaque sugarpaste, achieved from a simple sugar and water syrup. It can be made into a confection by cutting it into designs, shaping it into a menagerie of animals or a floral centrepiece, or simply rolling it into a smooth and delicious sheet to blanket a cake.

Fondant has a sweet taste that blends beautifully with fruits, nuts and chocolate, which means it can form the basis of many confections. The quantities of sugar and water you need will depend on the confection, but for 400g/14oz fondant, you will need 400g/14oz/2 cups caster (superfine) sugar and 150ml/ ¼ pint/⅔ cup water. You will need to start making this the day before you need to use it.

Below: Once made, fondant can be coloured and shaped.

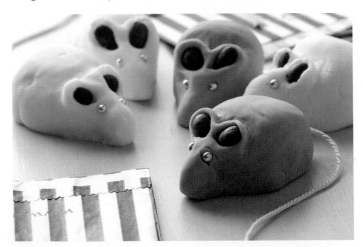

Making fondant

1 Dampen a marble slab, a metal scraper and a wooden spatula with cold water. Prepare an ice-water bath. Combine the quantities of sugar and water stated in the recipe in a large, heavy pan and heat until the sugar dissolves. Bring to the boil, then lower the heat and cook until it reaches the soft-ball stage (114°C/238°F). (See pages 14–15.)

2 Pour the syrup on to the prepared marble, and leave it to cool for 3 minutes. Arrest the cooking by placing the pan in the ice-water bath.

4 With the wooden spatula, work the syrup in a figure of eight movement for about 10 minutes, until thick and opaque.

6 When it is too firm to be worked with the scraper, gather it up into a ball. Moisten your hands with cold water and knead the fondant for 10 minutes until smooth.

3 Using the dampened metal scraper, begin to fold the edges into the centre of the pool, until the mixture becomes glossy.

5 Once the fondant is firmer and has become white, switch back to the metal scraper, moistened again with cold water, and continue to work the fondant for 10 minutes.

7 Place the fondant inside a dampened bowl. Cover with a damp, clean dish towel and chill overnight (or for at least 12 hours).

Working with Taffy

Whereas simple hard-boiled sweets are made from a simple sugar syrup heated to the hard-crack stage and then allowed to set in shapes, pulled taffies are heated to the soft-crack stage and then manipulated by pulling and stretching. Taffy can be coloured one colour or multiple colours, and can be moulded into various shapes.

Types of taffy

The way a sugar syrup is handled will dictate the texture of the finished taffy. Turning, pulling, stretching and manipulating the mixture between the hands incorporates tiny air bubbles. Depending on how firmly and for how long the mixture is turned and mixed, you can end up with a whole range of sweets, from hard, glossy candies such as bull's eyes and lemon drops to softer, chalky ones such as Edinburgh rock. Chewy taffies are taken to lower temperatures, which means that they do not set as hard sweets, but as soft and chewy delights. (Taffy should not be confused with toffee, which is an entirely different confection that has butter and cream added to the sugar syrup.)

Pulling taffy

1   As soon as the syrup has reached the temperature specified in the recipe, it should be poured out on to a pre-oiled marble worktop or other clean, smooth, dry work surface. Using an oiled metal scraper, turn the edges of the pool of syrup in on itself. This helps the syrup to cool evenly and begins the process of incorporating air.

2   Taffy must be handled quickly before it sets too hard, but be very careful that it does not burn your hands, as it will be very hot. Oil your hands, as well as the work surface, so that the sugar does not stick to them. Coax the syrup into a cylinder shape, then take each end and stretch it out. It will be very soft at first and may break. Do not worry about this – simply gather up the pieces and push them together again.

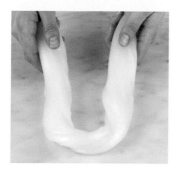

3 Stretch the taffy into a long rope and then bring the ends towards you to create a horseshoe shape.

4 Now grab the top of the horseshoe with one hand, and the bottom (where the two ends meet) with the other hand. Twist the ends in opposite directions, bringing the two sides together into one rope. Repeat the stretching and twisting process until the syrup begins to harden. Each individual recipe will give instructions as to the length of time for which you will need to work the taffy, as this varies depending on the texture of the confection. For harder sweets, it will be 15–20 minutes, for chewier taffies, it may be only 10 minutes. Once you have worked it for the required time, the taffy will be ready to be cut and shaped – this should be done immediately.

Cutting and shaping taffy

Taffy should be cut as soon as the pulling process is finished, or it will set too hard to shape. The best tool to use is a pair of oiled kitchen scissors. The pieces look like little pillows if left just as they are, such as in the Rose Water Edinburgh Rock recipe. Alternatively, they can be quickly rolled into balls or into shapes, as in the traditional Lemon Drops recipe.

Adding colour

• If the entire confection is to be one colour, fold a little colouring into the pool of syrup with the metal scraper.
• If the recipe calls for two colours, such as Rhubarb and Custards, separate the syrup on the marble slab. Place one piece in an oiled ovenproof dish, in a warm oven while the other piece is coloured and stretched. Then swap them over, and colour and stretch the second piece.

Storing taffies

• If you are not serving them immediately, wrap taffies individually in greaseproof (waxed) paper, baking parchment, cellophane or pretty foil wrappers.
• You can buy sweet wrappers from specialist stores or from on-line retailers.
• A candy dish or jar with a tight-fitting lid is ideal for storing the wrapped sweets, as they will soften in the open air.

Hard Candies and Lollipops

Everyone has a favourite boiled sweet or hard candy, and quite often it is one that has stuck with them since childhood. Whether it's a minty humbug, tangy sour drop or zesty lemon drop, a whole host of flavours can be added to a simple sugar syrup to create divine confections. This chapter contains all shapes and colours, from hand-moulded candy canes and little pillows of Edinburgh rock to divine lollipops, which are set on sticks.

Lemon Drops

Adorable miniature lemon-shaped drops are a classic sweet around the world. Opaque yellow with a sugary coating, they have a certain sparkle and should be put in beautiful little dishes to entice your family and friends to eat them.

Makes about 600g/1lb 6oz

grapeseed or groundnut (peanut)
  oil, for greasing
400g/14oz/2 cups caster
  (superfine) sugar
15ml/1 tbsp liquid glucose or
  golden (light corn) syrup
150ml/¼ pint/⅔ cup water
2.5ml/½ tsp lemon oil or
  5ml/1 tsp lemon extract
2 drops yellow food colouring
200g/7oz/1 cup caster sugar,
  for dusting

Cook's Tip
Be sure to use a high quality lemon extract or oil. Lemon extract is usually lemon oil diluted with water, so you will need to use double the quantity to get the strong lemony flavour.

1 Grease a marble slab, a metal scraper and a pair of scissors. Prepare an ice-water bath. Combine the sugar, liquid glucose or golden syrup, and water in a heavy pan and bring to the boil. Reduce the heat to medium and cook, without stirring, until the mixture reaches the soft-crack stage (143°C/290°F).

2 Remove the pan from the heat and stir in the lemon oil or extract and yellow food colouring. Stir until the mixture stops bubbling, then arrest the cooking by placing the pan in the ice-water bath.

3 Pour the syrup on to the marble slab and allow it to cool until a skin forms. Using the oiled scraper, fold the edges into the centre of the pool until it is cool enough to handle. Grease your hands with oil.

4 With the aid of the scraper, lift the syrup up off the marble and work it into a cylindrical shape. Pull it from either end to make a long strand. Take hold of the ends of the strand and pull them up toward you to form a 'U' shape. Twist the two sides into a rope, then pull from both ends into a 'U' shape.

5 Repeat these steps for about 15–20 minutes, until the syrup rope becomes opaque and a lot lighter in colour. You need to keep working it constantly so that it remains supple. If it becomes too hard, you can put it in a cool oven for a few minutes until it softens enough to work with again.

6 Gently pull it into a long, thin strand, then fold it in half and then in half again, to create four even lengths. Twist them up into a rope and pull until the diameter is 2cm/1in. Use oiled scissors to cut it into small pieces. Roll the pieces into little ovals using oiled hands and pinch each end into a point.

7 Dust the lemon drops in caster sugar to coat. Serve immediately, or wrap in baking parchment or waxed paper and store in an airtight container.

Energy 2412kcal/10289kJ; Protein 3g; Carbohydrate 639.7g, of which sugars 633g; Fat 0g, of which saturates 0g; Cholesterol 0mg; Calcium 319mg; Fibre 0g; Sodium 59mg

Pear Drops

These simple drops look especially pretty when poured into little moulds. If you can get your hands on an antique mould, use that. Otherwise, pour them out free-form on to an oiled marble slab or baking sheet. Pear drops are a traditional favourite in many countries.

Makes about 600g/1lb 6oz

grapeseed or groundnut (peanut) oil, for greasing
450g/1lb/2¼ cups caster (superfine) sugar
50ml/2fl oz/1¼ cup water
175ml/6fl oz/¾ cup pear juice
1.25ml/¼ tsp cream of tartar
30ml/2 tbsp lime juice
1 drop green food colouring

Variation
Pour the mixture into an oiled Swiss roll tin (jelly roll pan). Once set, drop the tin on the counter to shatter it.

1 Grease a sweet or candy mould, or a baking sheet, with the oil. Prepare an ice-water bath or fill the sink with a little cold water.

2 Put the sugar, water, 150ml/¼ pint/⅔ cup of the pear juice, and the cream of tartar in a heavy pan. Heat over a moderate heat until the sugar has dissolved.

3 Turn the heat up to high and boil until it reaches the soft-ball stage (114°C/238°F). Add the lime juice, the rest of the pear juice and the food colouring. Do not stir as this could cause it to crystallize.

4 Bring back to the boil. Cook until it reaches the hard-crack stage (154°C/310°F). Remove from the heat and place over the cold water to arrest the cooking.

5 Spoon immediately into the mould or drop spoonfuls on to the baking sheet. Cool completely. Remove the sweets with the tip of a knife. Serve immediately, or wrap in baking parchment or waxed paper and store in an airtight container.

Energy 1841kcal/7860kJ; Protein 2.4g; Carbohydrate 488.1g, of which sugars 488.1g; Fat 0.2g, of which saturates 0g; Cholesterol 0mg; Calcium 251mg; Fibre 0g; Sodium 31mg

Sour Drops

People either love or hate sour sweets. For me, there is nothing more satisfying than a hard, sugary sweet with a mouth-puckering tang. Sour drops were originally called 'acidulated drops' in 19-century Britain. They are also known as acid drops and sourballs.

Makes about 600g/1lb 6oz

grapeseed or groundnut (peanut)
  oil, for greasing
450g/1lb/2¼ cups caster
  (superfine) sugar
150ml/¼ pint/⅔ cup water
2.5ml/½ tsp cream of tartar
2.5ml/½ tsp lemon juice
5ml/1 tsp tartaric acid
icing (confectioners') sugar,
  for dusting

Cook's Tip
Although it sounds like a chemical, tartaric acid is actually an organic by-product of winemaking. If you cannot find tartaric acid, you can use citric acid instead. Websites that sell home brewing kits usually sell tartaric acid.

1   Grease a marble slab. Prepare an ice-water bath or fill the sink with a little cold water.

2   Put the sugar, water and cream of tartar in a heavy pan over a moderate heat, and leave for about 5 minutes until the sugar has dissolved.

3   Turn the heat up to high and boil the mixture until it begins to turn yellow in colour and reaches the soft-ball stage (116°C/240°F).

4   Add the lemon juice to the syrup, but resist the temptation to stir it, as this could cause the syrup to crystallize. Continue boiling until it reaches the hard-crack stage (154°C/310°F), then remove from the heat. Place the pan briefly over the ice-water bath or cold water to arrest the cooking.

5   Sprinkle over the tartaric acid and quickly stir it into the syrup.

6   Holding the pan of syrup low over the marble, carefully pour it out in drops about the size of a large coin, or spoon it on to the marble. Allow to harden.

7   Using an offset spatula, loosen the discs from the marble. Dust with icing sugar, then shake off any excess. Serve immediately, or wrap in baking parchment or waxed paper and store in an airtight container.

Energy 1862kcal/7984kJ; Protein 1g; Carbohydrate 476g, of which sugars 475g; Fat 0g, of which saturates 0g; Cholesterol 0mg; Calcium 59mg; Fibre 0g; Sodium 25mg

Rhubarb and Custards

Inspired by a dessert made from stewed rhubarb and custard that was once common in schools, these iconic two-tone treats are one of the most popular British boiled sweets. Using two colours requires a preheated oven so that you can keep the unworked syrup warm.

Makes about 600g/1lb 6oz

grapeseed or groundnut (peanut) oil, for greasing
450g/1lb/2¼ cups granulated (white) sugar, plus extra for dusting
150ml/¼ pint/⅔ cup water
1.5ml/¼ tsp cream of tartar
15ml/1 tbsp golden (light corn) syrup
10ml/2 tsp tartaric acid
½ vanilla pod (bean), scraped
2–3 drops pink food colouring

Variation
Traditionally these are made without vanilla, but the addition of fresh vanilla balances the flavours well. You could omit the vanilla, if you like, or use 2 drops of vanilla extract instead.

1 Grease a marble slab, a metal scraper and a pair of kitchen scissors. Prepare an ice-water bath. Preheat the oven to 150°C/300°F/Gas 2.
2 Combine the sugar, water, cream of tartar and golden syrup in a heavy pan, and stir to dissolve the sugar. Bring to the boil, then reduce the heat to medium and cook, without stirring, until it reaches the soft-crack stage (143°C/290°F). Add the tartaric acid and swirl the pan around.
3 Place the pan in the ice-water bath to arrest the cooking, then pour the syrup on to the marble. Leave to cool until a skin forms. Using the scraper, cut off half the syrup and place it back in the pan. Place the pan in the oven.
4 Using the scraper, fold the edges into the centre of the remaining syrup until it is cool enough to handle. Add the vanilla seeds. Oil your hands and, with the aid of the scraper, lift the syrup up off the marble and work it into a cylinder, mixing the vanilla seeds in as you go. Pull it into a long strand.
5 Take hold of the ends of the syrup strand and pull them up towards you to form a 'U' shape. Twist the two sides together into a rope, then pull again from both ends to make the 'U' shape. Repeat for 15–20 minutes, until the syrup rope becomes opaque and a lot lighter in colour. Work it constantly so that it remains supple. (If it becomes hard, put it in the oven to soften.)
6 Remove the un-pulled piece of syrup from the pan and replace it with the vanilla piece. Working quickly, add the pink colouring to the unworked syrup with the scraper, and form it into a thick log. Press the vanilla piece alongside the pink one. Pull at both ends, until the strand is 1cm/½in thick. Cool slightly.
7 Using oiled scissors, cut into pieces. Toss in sugar. Serve immediately, or wrap in baking parchment or waxed paper and store in an airtight container.

Energy 2015kcal/8595kJ; Protein 2.5g; Carbohydrate 534.4g, of which sugars 534.4g; Fat 0g, of which saturates 0g; Cholesterol 0mg; Calcium 269mg; Fibre 0g; Sodium 71mg

Bull's Eyes

Another Victorian-era confection, bull's eyes are slightly sour because of the addition of tartaric acid, which contrasts well with the deep caramel taste of the brown sugar. Pulling half of the mixture and leaving the rest brown creates the two colours.

Makes about 600g/1lb 6oz

grapeseed or groundnut (peanut) oil, for greasing
425g/15oz/scant 2 cups soft dark brown sugar
75ml/5 tbsp water
0.75ml/⅛ tsp cream of tartar
2.5ml/½ tsp lemon extract
0.75ml/⅛ tsp tartaric acid or citric acid

Cook's Tip
You need to work the syrup constantly so that it remains supple. If it becomes too hard, put it in the oven until it softens.

1 Grease a marble slab, a metal scraper and a pair of kitchen scissors. Prepare an ice-water bath. Preheat the oven to 150°C/300°F/Gas 2.
2 Combine the sugar, water, and cream of tartar in a heavy pan. Heat gently until the sugar dissolves, then bring to the boil. Reduce the heat to medium and cook, without stirring, until it reaches the soft-crack stage (143°C/290°F). Add the lemon extract and tartaric acid or citric acid, then arrest the cooking by setting the pan into the ice-water bath. Pour the syrup on to the oiled marble slab and allow it to cool until a skin forms.
3 Using the oiled scraper, cut off one-third of the syrup and put it back into the pan. Place the pan in the warm oven to prevent the syrup from hardening. Using the scraper, fold the edges of the remaining syrup into the centre, until it is cool enough to handle. Oil your hands and, with the aid of the scraper, lift the syrup off the marble and work it into a cylinder. Pull it into a long strand.
4 Take hold of the ends of the syrup strand and pull them up toward you to form a 'U' shape. Twist the two sides together into a rope, then pull from both ends to make the 'U' shape. Repeat for 15–20 minutes, until opaque.
5 Gently pull the syrup into a flat rectangle and place it on the marble slab. Remove the smaller portion of syrup from the pan and roll it into a sausage shape that is the length of the rectangle. Place it on one side of the rectangle. Roll the rectangle around it, so the darker syrup is enclosed.
6 Hold the ends and pull as before, to form a 'U', then twist and pull into a long 2cm/¾in wide rope. Using oiled scissors, cut it into pieces. With oiled hands, roll the pieces into little balls. Serve immediately, or wrap in baking parchment or waxed paper and store in an airtight container.

Energy 1644kcal/7018kJ; Protein 0g; Carbohydrate 456g, of which sugars 456g; Fat 0g, of which saturates 0g; Cholesterol 0mg; Calcium 252mg; Fibre 0g; Sodium 140mg

Peppermint Humbugs

'Humbug', meaning a hoax or hypocrite, was a term used frequently in the 18th and 19th centuries, most famously by Charles Dickens in A Christmas Carol. The sweet was perhaps given the name because of the unexpected intensity of flavour, which belies its appearance.

Makes about 600g/1lb 6oz

grapeseed or groundnut (peanut) oil, for greasing
450g/1lb/2¼ cups granulated (white) sugar
150ml/¼ pint/⅔ cup water
1.5ml/¼ tsp cream of tartar
15ml/1 tbsp golden (light corn) syrup
10ml/2 tsp peppermint extract
2–3 drops black food colouring

1 Grease a marble slab, a metal scraper and a pair of kitchen scissors. Prepare an ice-water bath. Preheat the oven to 150°C/300°F/Gas 2.
2 Combine the sugar, water, cream of tartar and golden syrup in a heavy pan. Heat gently until the sugar dissolves, then bring to the boil. Reduce the heat to medium and cook, without stirring, until it reaches the soft-crack stage (143°C/290°F). Add the peppermint extract. Place the pan in the ice-water bath. Pour the syrup on to the marble slab and leave to cool until a skin forms.
3 Using the oiled scraper, cut off one-third of the syrup and place it back in the pan. Place the pan in the warm oven. Using the scraper, fold the edges of the remaining syrup into the centre until cool enough to handle.
4 Oil your hands and, with the aid of the scraper, lift the syrup off the marble and work it into a cylindrical shape. Pull it from both ends to form a long strand. Take hold of the ends of the syrup strand and pull them up toward you to form a 'U' shape. Twist the two sides together into a rope, then pull again from both ends to make the 'U' shape. Repeat for 15–20 minutes, until opaque.
5 Divide the pulled syrup into four pieces and pull these to form strands of equal length and thickness. Remove the un-pulled piece of syrup from the pan. Working quickly, add the black colouring to it with the scraper, and shape it into a log that is the same length as the white pieces but thicker.
6 Press the white ropes alongside the black log, spacing them around the central black piece. Pull the whole thing gently at both ends until it is 1cm/½in thick. Twist it so that the white spirals around the black. Cut into pieces.
7 Serve immediately, or wrap in baking parchment or waxed paper and store in an airtight container.

Energy 1621kcal/6914kJ; Protein 2g; Carbohydrate 429.9g, of which sugars 429.9g; Fat 0g, of which saturates 0g; Cholesterol 0mg; Calcium 216mg; Fibre 0g; Sodium 65mg

Aniseed Twists

Also known as anise candy, these little, hard twists have a wonderful depth of flavour. They can be made with anise extract for a smooth consistency, or you can use fresh aniseed, which is a great alternative – the tiny, flavourful seeds give a nice contrast to the sweetness.

Makes about 600g/1lb 6oz

grapeseed or groundnut (peanut) oil, for greasing
400g/14oz/2 cups caster (superfine) sugar
100ml/3½fl oz/scant ½ cup water
100ml/3½fl oz/scant ½ cup liquid glucose or golden (light corn) syrup
15ml/1 tbsp red food colouring or 3 drops concentrated colour paste or gel
15ml/1 tbsp pulverized aniseed or 10ml/2 tsp anise extract

1 Grease a marble slab, a metal scraper and a pair of kitchen scissors. Prepare an ice-water bath.
2 Combine the sugar, water and liquid glucose or golden syrup in a heavy pan and heat gently until the sugar dissolves. Bring to the boil, then reduce the heat to medium and cook, without stirring, until the mixture reaches the soft-crack stage (143°C/290°F). Add the food colouring and aniseed or anise extract. Arrest the cooking by placing the pan in the ice-water bath.
3 Pour on to the marble slab. Allow to cool until a skin forms. Using the oiled scraper, fold the edges into the centre of the pool until cool enough to handle.
4 Oil your hands and, with the aid of the scraper, lift the syrup off the marble and work it into a cylinder. Pull it out from both ends to make a long, thick strand. Take hold of the ends of the syrup strand and pull them up towards you to form a 'U' shape. Twist the two sides together into a rope. Continue to stretch the rope, twisting all the time, until it is 1cm/½in thick. Working quickly, use oiled scissors to cut the strand into even, bitesize pieces. Wrap in cellophane.

Cook's Tip
If not serving immediately, store in an airtight container.

Energy 1894kcal/8079kJ; Protein 2g; Carbohydrate 502.7g, of which sugars 458.2g; Fat 0g, of which saturates 0g; Cholesterol 0mg; Calcium 220mg; Fibre 0g; Sodium 17mg

Barley Sugar Sticks

Barley sugar was originally made with the water left over from cooking pearl barley, but it is essentially a hard-boiled sweet flavoured with lemon. You could try making them using the strained cooking water from boiled pearl barley, if you like. The flavour will be rich and earthy.

Makes about 600g/1lb 6oz

grapeseed or groundnut (peanut) oil, for greasing
450g/1lb/2¼ cups granulated (white) sugar
150ml/¼ pint/⅔ cup water
thinly peeled rind of 1 lemon
1.5ml/¼ tsp cream of tartar
juice of ½ lemon

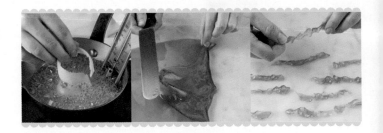

1   Grease a marble slab, a palette knife or metal spatula, and a pair of kitchen scissors. Prepare an ice-water bath.

2   Place the sugar and water in a heavy pan and bring to the boil. Add the lemon rind and cream of tartar. Boil the syrup until it reaches the soft-ball stage (114°C/238°F). Add the lemon juice, then continue to boil until it reaches the hard-crack stage (154°C/310°F).

3   Remove the pan from the heat and place it momentarily over the ice-water bath. Remove the lemon rind with a fork and discard.

4   Pour the syrup on to the marble and allow to cool for 1 minute. Using the oiled palette knife or metal spatula, fold each side into the centre of the pool.

5   Gently pull the two ends to make a longer, thinner, flat piece of syrup. Using oiled scissors, cut 1cm/½in strips.

6   Working quickly, twist the strips into corkscrew shapes. Serve immediately, or wrap the sweets in baking parchment or waxed paper and store in an airtight container.

Energy 1777kcal/7579kJ; Protein 0g; Carbohydrate 473g, of which sugars 473g; Fat 0g, of which saturates 0g; Cholesterol 0mg; Calcium 47mg; Fibre 0g; Sodium 23mg

Candy Canes

These colourful confections are fun to create and make great holiday gifts. They can be used to decorate a Christmas tree, adding the finishing festive touch. This recipe uses peppermint extract and red food colouring, but you could experiment with other colours and flavours.

Makes about 600g/1lb 6oz

grapeseed or groundnut (peanut) oil, for greasing
450g/1lb/2¼ cups granulated (white) sugar
150ml/¼ pint/⅔ cup water
1.5ml/¼ tsp cream of tartar
15ml/1 tbsp golden (light corn) syrup
10ml/2 tsp peppermint extract
2–3 drops red food colouring

1 Grease a marble slab, a metal scraper and a pair of kitchen scissors. Prepare an ice-water bath. Preheat the oven to 150°C/300°F/Gas 2.
2 Combine the sugar, water, cream of tartar and golden syrup in a heavy pan, and stir over a medium heat until the sugar has dissolved. Bring to the boil. Reduce the heat and cook, without stirring, until it reaches the soft-crack stage (143°C/290°F). Add the peppermint extract. Place the base of the pan in the ice-water bath, then pour the syrup on to the oiled marble slab and allow it to cool until a skin forms on the surface.
3 Using the oiled scraper, cut off half the syrup and place it back in the pan. Place the pan in the warm oven. Using the oiled scraper, begin to fold the edges of the remaining syrup into the centre until it is cool enough to handle.
4 Oil your hands and, with the aid of the scraper, lift the syrup off the marble and work it into a cylinder. Pull it from both ends to make a long strand.
5 Take hold of the ends and pull them up toward you to form a 'U' shape. Twist the two sides together into a rope, then pull again from both ends to make the 'U' shape. Repeat for 15–20 minutes, until it is opaque.
6 Remove the un-pulled syrup from the pan. Place the pulled piece in the pan. Working quickly, add the red colouring to the unworked syrup with the scraper. Work the red syrup into a log the same length as the white piece. Press the white syrup alongside the red piece. Pull the whole thing gently until 1cm/½in thick. Twist to create a swirl pattern. Leave to cool slightly.
7 Using oiled scissors, cut it into long, even lengths, and bend a curve in the top of each, to form canes. Leave to harden. Serve immediately, or wrap in baking parchment or waxed paper and store in an airtight container.

Energy 1775kcal/7570kJ; Protein 0g; Carbohydrate 473g, of which sugars 473g; Fat 0g, of which saturates 0g; Cholesterol 0mg; Calcium 45mg; Fibre 0g; Sodium 23mg

Rose Water Edinburgh Rock

Edinburgh rock was one of those cooking mishaps that turned into a triumph. It is nothing like conventional British rock. The story goes that some boiled sweets were exposed to air overnight, and as a result went soft and powdery, causing a revelation. These can be made in any flavour.

Makes about 675g/1½lb

grapeseed or groundnut (peanut) oil, for greasing
450g/1lb/2¼ cups granulated (white) sugar
15ml/1 tbsp liquid glucose or golden (light corn) syrup
2.5ml/½ tsp cream of tartar
200ml/7fl oz/scant 1 cup water
10ml/2 tsp pink food colouring, or 2 drops concentrated colour paste or gel
10ml/2 tsp rose water
icing (confectioners') sugar, for dusting

1　Grease a marble slab, a metal scraper and a pair of kitchen scissors. Prepare an ice-water bath.
2　Combine the sugar, liquid glucose or golden syrup, cream of tartar and water in a heavy pan. Heat gently over medium heat until the sugar dissolves. Bring it to the boil. Cook until it reaches the soft-crack stage (143°C/290°F).
3　Stir in the colouring and rose water, and immediately place the pan in the ice-water bath. Pour the syrup on to the oiled marble slab and allow it to cool until a skin forms. Using the scraper, fold the edges into the centre until cool enough to handle. Dust your hands with icing sugar.
4　Lift the syrup and form it into a cylinder. Take hold of the ends and pull them toward you to form a 'U' shape. Press the two sides together and form it into the 'U' shape again. Do not twist it. Continue for 10 minutes until opaque.
5　Pull it into a long strip, then cut it into small pieces with scissors. Leave it out at room temperature for 24 hours, until soft and powdery. Serve immediately, or store in an airtight container after that.

Energy 1821kcal/7768kJ; Protein 2.3g; Carbohydrate 483g, of which sugars 476.3g; Fat 0g, of which saturates 0g; Cholesterol 0mg; Calcium 240mg; Fibre 0g; Sodium 50mg

Raspberry Lollipops

Fruit juice lollipops are one of the best ways to preserve the natural flavour of perfectly ripe berries. These raspberry lollipops have a wonderful colour, and taste even better than they look. Experiment with different berries to make a range of fun and delicious lollipops.

Makes about 675g/1½lb

grapeseed or groundnut (peanut)
   oil, for greasing
300g/11oz/2 cups raspberries
400g/14oz/2 cups caster
   (superfine) sugar

1   Grease a baking sheet and prepare an ice-water bath. Put the raspberries in a heavy pan, and heat gently until the fruits have softened and the juices have run. Do not stir.

2   Strain through a sieve (strainer) placed over a large bowl to catch the juices. Resist the temptation to push the berries through the sieve with a spoon or other implement, as this will cause the juice to go cloudy.

3   Put the sugar in a heavy pan and add the strained raspberry juice. Stir over medium heat until the sugar has dissolved, then bring to the boil.

4   Boil, without stirring, over medium heat until the syrup reaches the hard-crack stage (154°C/310°F). Do not stir. If sugar crystals form around the edge of the pan, use a dampened pastry or silicone brush to coax them back into the syrup. Arrest the cooking by placing the pan in the ice-bath.

5   Pour spoonfuls of the syrup on to the prepared baking sheet, about 5cm/2in apart. Press lollipop sticks into the syrup. Pour another drop of syrup over the top of the stick to seal it in. Allow to cool completely.

6   Removing them from the paper and wrap individually in cellophane.

Energy 1651kcal/7051kJ; Protein 6.2g; Carbohydrate 432g, of which sugars 432g; Fat 1g, of which saturates 0.3g; Cholesterol 0mg; Calcium 287mg; Fibre 7.5g; Sodium 33mg

Jewelled Lollipops

Lollipops are always popular with children. They are usually round or oval-shaped and come in many colours. These beautiful jewelled ones are wonderfully simple to make, using pretty dried fruits and nuts for texture and decoration. You can use whatever fruits and nuts you like.

Makes 12

grapeseed or groundnut (peanut)
  oil, for greasing
100ml/3½fl oz/scant ½ cup
  water
400g/14oz/2 cups caster
  (superfine) sugar
15ml/1 tbsp liquid glucose
  or 5ml/1 tsp cream of tartar
40g/1½oz/¼ cup assorted dried
  fruits, such as cranberries,
  sultanas (golden raisins)
  and chopped apricots
25g/1oz/3 tbsp shelled
  pistachio nuts

1 Grease a marble slab or baking sheet, or line it with a silicone mat. Put the water, sugar and liquid glucose or cream of tartar in a large, heavy pan. Stir over medium heat until the sugar has dissolved.

2 Prepare an ice-water bath. Boil the syrup, without stirring, until it reaches the hard-crack stage (154°C/310°F). Immediately place the pan in an ice-water bath to arrest the cooking.

3 Spoon 12 circles of syrup on to the prepared surface, reserving about one-fifth of the syrup. Working quickly, press a lollipop stick into each lollipop, then pour a drop of the remaining syrup over the top of each stick to seal it in. Press in the dried fruits and nuts to make a random pattern.

4 Leave the lollipops to harden for 10 minutes, then remove them carefully from the surface by holding on to the stick; go slowly, they will release eventually.

5 Serve immediately, or wrap in baking parchment or waxed paper and store for a few days in an airtight container.

Energy 1884kcal/8016kJ; Protein 7.2g; Carbohydrate 460.8g, of which sugars 453.6g; Fat 14.4g, of which saturates 2.4g; Cholesterol 0mg; Calcium 264mg; Fibre 2.4g; Sodium 192mg

Fruit Sherbet

Here is a delicious dip to accompany your homemade lollipops. Recreate a childhood classic combination by making the Raspberry Lollipops on page 42, to dip in the powder. This combination evokes nostalgia on both sides of the Atlantic.

Makes 500g/1¼ lb

500g/1¼lb/2½ cups caster (superfine) sugar
15ml/1 tbsp tartaric acid or citric acid
10–12 drops lemon or orange extract
1–2 drops yellow or orange food colouring

Cook's Tip
To make a tasty drink, simply combine 5–10ml/ 1–2 tsp of the powder with a glass of water.

1 Place the caster sugar in the bowl of a food processor or blender, and process or blend until the sugar is in extremely fine crystals. This should take a few minutes.

2 Transfer the sugar to a large mixing bowl, and add the tartaric acid or citric acid, and the lemon or orange extract.

3 Add the yellow or orange food colouring to the sugar.

4 Mix well with a wooden spoon or spatula until the food colouring is evenly distributed throughout the sugar and you have achieved an even shade. This may take a few minutes.

5 Leave the sherbet to dry before storing in an airtight container. Serve in little bags for dipping lollipops into, or alternatively use the powder to make a refreshing drink (see Cook's Tip).

Energy 1970kcal/8405kJ; Protein 2.5g; Carbohydrate 522.5g, of which sugars 522.5g; Fat 0g, of which saturates 0g; Cholesterol 0mg; Calcium 265mg; Fibre 0g; Sodium 30mg

Chews and Fondants

This chapter contains a selection of soft and chewy delights from around the world, perfect for giving your jaw a good workout. From traditional salt-water taffy to adorable fondant mice, there are morsels here to please people of all ages – from small children to grandparents and including every family member in-between. There are all kinds of tempting ideas for using fondant, including colouring, flavouring and shaping it to create different effects and tastes.

Salt-Water Taffy

Supposedly made with sea water, salt-water taffy is originally from Atlantic City, though you used to be able to find it along the boardwalks at most American seaside towns. Soft, chewy and a little salty, it is the perfect treat. You will need greaseproof (waxed) paper for wrapping.

Makes about 400g/14oz

grapeseed or groundnut (peanut)
  oil, for greasing
200g/7oz/1 cup caster
  (superfine) or granulated
  (white) sugar
15ml/1 tbsp cornflour (cornstarch)
150ml/¼ pint/⅔ cup liquid
  glucose or golden
  (light corn) syrup
25g/1oz/2 tbsp unsalted butter
120ml/4fl oz/½ cup water
1.5ml/¼ tsp sea salt

1 Grease a marble slab, a metal scraper and a pair of kitchen scissors.
2 Combine the sugar and cornflour in a large, heavy pan. Add the liquid glucose or golden syrup, butter, water and salt. Heat gently until the sugar dissolves, then boil until it reaches the hard-ball stage (130°C/266°F).
3 Pour the taffy on to the prepared marble slab. Allow to cool for a few minutes until it can be handled. Oil your hands and, with the aid of the scraper, lift the syrup off the marble slab and work it into a cylinder.
4 Pull the syrup out from both ends to make a long, thick strand. Take hold of the ends of the strand and pull them toward you to form a 'U' shape.
5 Twist the two sides into a rope, then continue in this way, twisting the whole time, for 10 minutes, until it is lighter and firm enough to hold a shape. Stretch the strand until it is 2.5cm/1in in diameter.
6 Using oiled scissors, cut the strand into bitesize pieces. Wrap in greaseproof (waxed) paper and twist the ends to seal. Serve immediately, or store in an airtight container.

Variation

Add food colouring or flavours to the syrup just as it reaches the hard-ball stage. Traditionally, it comes in pastel shades.

Energy 1502kcal/6378kJ; Protein 1.2g; Carbohydrate 350g, of which sugars 269.3g; Fat 21g, of which saturates 14g; Cholesterol 58mg; Calcium 124mg; Fibre 0g; Sodium 1022mg

Honey and Star Anise Chews

Star anise is usually found whole, but it is easily ground in a coffee grinder or blender. It adds depth of flavour to these simple chews, and combines perfectly with the honey and sesame seeds. Choose any variety of honey you like – each type will give a slightly different taste.

Makes about 25

50g/2oz/4 tbsp sesame seeds
225ml/7½fl oz/scant 1 cup
  honey
6ml/1¼ tsp ground star anise
  (see Cook's Tip)

Cook's Tip
Grinding your own spices gives more flavour, but the aroma can linger. To clean a spice grinder, wash it with warm soapy water and dry it well. Place a little stale bread in the grinder and whizz it around. It will gather most of the residual scent.

1 Place a dry frying pan over medium heat. When it gets hot, add the sesame seeds. Watch them carefully, as they burn easily. Toss the sesame seeds around until they are a light golden brown, but not too dark. Transfer them to a small bowl.
2 Place about 25 mini cake or sweet cases on a baking sheet and set aside.
3 In a small pan, cook the honey and star anise together over a low heat until the mixture reaches the firm-ball stage (120°C/248°F).
4 When the honey reaches the firm-ball stage, remove it from the heat and spoon it into the prepared cases.
5 Leave to cool, then sprinkle with the sesame seeds. Serve immediately or store in an airtight container.

Energy 950kcal/4000kJ; Protein 0g; Carbohydrate 175g, of which sugars 175g; Fat 25g, of which saturates 0g; Cholesterol 0mg; Calcium 375mg; Fibre 0g; Sodium 25mg

Maple Cream Candy

Walnuts and maple syrup are wonderful together, though if you prefer a creamy maple candy with no nuts, you can omit them. These candies have a soft, chewy consistency, and are particularly popular in North America, where maple syrup is a much-loved ingredient.

Makes about 675g/1½lb

400g/14oz/2 cups granulated (white) sugar
225g/8oz/⅔ cup maple syrup
120ml/4fl oz/½ cup double (heavy) cream
120ml/4fl oz/½ cup water
1 vanilla pod (bean)
25g/1oz/2 tbsp unsalted butter, plus extra for greasing
40g/1½oz/⅓ cup walnuts, finely chopped
2.5ml/½ tsp salt
about 25 walnut halves

1 Place about 25 mini cake or sweet cases on a baking sheet. Alternatively, grease a 20cm/8in square cake tin (pan) and line it with baking parchment.
2 Combine the sugar, maple syrup, cream and water in a heavy pan. Split the vanilla pod and scrape the seeds into the pan. Add the pod, too. Place over a medium heat and stir until the sugar has dissolved.
3 Bring to the boil, then boil, without stirring, until the mixture reaches the soft-ball stage (114°C/238°F). Add the butter and stir to combine. Pour the mixture into a shallow bowl and leave to cool to 43°C/110°F.
4 Beat the syrup with a wooden spoon until it is light and fluffy (alternatively, use an electric mixer). Stir in the nuts and salt.
5 Press the mixture into the cake cases or the prepared tin. If using a tin, score the surface to create about 25 portions. Top each with a walnut half. Leave to go cold, then cut along the markings.
6 Serve immediately, or store in an airtight container for a few days.

Energy 3773kcal/15818kJ; Protein 20g; Carbohydrate 577g, of which sugars 562g; Fat 168g, of which saturates 60g; Cholesterol 222mg; Calcium 366mg; Fibre 7g; Sodium 1060mg

Pineapple Chews

For the best flavour, use a good quality candied pineapple to make these fruity morsels.
The rum adds a lovely depth to the chews and cuts the sweetness. Be sure to use a white rum,
as dark, spiced rum would overwhelm the pineapple flavour.

Makes 36

25g/1oz/2 tbsp unsalted butter,
  plus extra for greasing
300g/11oz/1½ cups caster
  (superfine) sugar
120ml/4fl oz/½ cup full-fat
  (whole) milk
185g/6½oz candied pineapple,
  chopped, plus 50g/2oz
  candied pineapple, cut into
  36 small wedges
25g/1oz white chocolate,
  chopped
2.5ml/½ tsp lemon juice
2.5ml/½ tsp white rum

1 Grease an 18cm/7in square baking tin (pan) and line with baking
parchment or waxed paper.
2 Put the butter, caster sugar and milk in a large, heavy pan. Cook over a
moderate heat, stirring constantly, until the sugar has dissolved and the
butter has melted.
3 Bring the mixture to the boil and cook until it reaches the soft-ball stage
(114°C/238°F). Remove from the heat.
4 Add the chopped pineapple, white chocolate, lemon juice and rum.
5 Leave the mixture to cool slightly, then stir it twice. Leave it for
1–2 minutes to cool a bit further, then stir it twice more. Continue in
this way, allowing it to cool between stirs. As it cools, it will thicken.
6 Transfer the fudge to the tin and press it down with an offset spatula.
Press the 36 candied pineapple wedges on to the surface, evenly
spacing them in rows of 6. Score the surface with a sharp knife and leave
to set completely.
7 Cut into 36 pieces. Serve immediately, or store in an airtight container.

Energy 2196kcal/9324kJ; Protein 7.2g; Carbohydrate 496.8g, of which sugars 496.8g; Fat 32.4g, of which saturates 21.6g; Cholesterol 72mg;
Calcium 468mg; Fibre 0g; Sodium 324mg

Fondant-stuffed Pecans

These traditional sweets are delicious and beautiful. The hard caramel shell glistens in the sunlight and sparkles in candlelight, so whether you take them to a picnic or present them after supper, they will impress. Display them in paper cases and pack them in little gift boxes.

Makes about 900g/2lb

750g/1lb 11oz/3¾ cups caster (superfine) sugar
200ml/7fl oz/scant 1 cup water
200g/7oz/2 cups pecan halves
15ml/1 tbsp Grand Marnier or Cointreau
finely grated rind of 1 orange
1.5ml/¼ tsp cream of tartar
icing (confectioners') sugar, for dusting

1 Dampen a marble slab, a metal scraper and a wooden spatula with cold water. Prepare an ice-water bath.

2 Follow the instructions on pages 16–17 for making fondant, using 400g/14oz/2 cups of the caster sugar and 150ml/¼ pint/⅔ cup of the water. Allow it to rest in the refrigerator for 12 hours.

3 Check through the pecan halves, setting aside any that are broken or unattractive for another recipe. Line a baking tray with baking parchment.

4 Add the liqueur and orange rind to the fondant, and knead the fondant until incorporated.

5 Dust your hands with icing sugar, then break off small pieces of fondant and roll them into small balls. Press a pecan on either side of the fondant, and place on the baking tray.

6 Prepare an ice-water bath. Combine the remaining caster sugar and water in a heavy pan with the cream of tartar, then heat gently. Stir until the sugar has dissolved, then cook, without stirring, until the mixture becomes a caramel colour. As soon as it reaches the right colour, arrest the cooking by placing the pan briefly in the ice-water bath.

7 Drop a few fondant balls at a time into the syrup, lifting out with a fork and placing on a cooling rack positioned over a piece of baking parchment to catch the drips. (You could place them directly on to the baking parchment, but this will leave the candies with a little 'foot' of caramel.)

8 After about an hour, the caramel will have hardened and the balls can be placed into individual mini cupcake or truffle cases and served. They will keep in an airtight container for a few days.

Energy 4377kcal/18445kJ; Protein 29g; Carbohydrate 799g, of which sugars 798g; Fat 137g, of which saturates 11g; Cholesterol 0mg; Calcium 263mg; Fibre 12g; Sodium 52mg

Lemon Cream Dreams

Soft, lemony, chewy morsels, these are wonderful sweets for sunny afternoons. They can be served at a tea party, or wrapped in squares of baking parchment, once cool, to pack for picnics. The fondant needs to chill overnight, so start the day before you need them.

Makes 25–30

400g/14oz/2 cups caster (superfine) sugar
150ml/½ pint/⅔ cup water
60ml/4 tbsp lemon juice
finely grated rind of 1 lemon
50g/2oz candied lemon peel
25g/1oz/¼ cup chopped pistachios

1 Dampen a marble slab, metal scraper and wooden spatula with cold water. Prepare an ice-water bath.

2 Follow the instructions on pages 16–17 for making fondant, using the 400g/14oz/2 cups caster sugar and 150ml/¼ pint/⅔ cup water. Allow it to rest in the refrigerator for 12 hours.

3 Set out 25–30 mini cake cases on a baking sheet. Chop the candied lemon peel.

4 Place the fondant in a heatproof bowl over a pan of barely simmering water. The water should reach the same level as the fondant in the bowl. Stir until just melted, then add the lemon juice and rind. If you melt it too much, it will go clear and then never set.

5 Pour the melted fondant into the mini cake cases, and sprinkle with the chopped peel and pistachios. Leave to cool at room temperature, then serve. These can be stored in an airtight container for a few days.

Energy 1860kcal/7860kJ; Protein 6g; Carbohydrate 450g, of which sugars 450g; Fat 15g, of which saturates 3g; Cholesterol 0mg; Calcium 300mg; Fibre 3g; Sodium 300mg

Sugar Mice

Sugar mice are traditionally found in the Christmas stockings of British children. These are formed from soft fondant and easy to make at home. Be creative with the decoration – small sweets or candies could be used instead of coffee beans, if you prefer.

Makes 6

400g/14oz/2 cups caster
  (superfine) sugar
150ml/½ pint/⅔ cup water
a few drops of pink food
  colouring
12 coffee beans
silver balls or other decorations,
  for the eyes
string, for the tail

Cook's Tip

If you would like to add whiskers to your mice, cut the bristles from a new (but inexpensive) pastry brush and push them into place with a wooden skewer or sugar working tool.
If you want edible whiskers and tail, try using thin liquorice laces.

1   Dampen a marble slab, metal scraper and wooden spatula with cold water. Prepare an ice-water bath.
2   Follow the instructions on pages 16–17 for making fondant, using the 400g/14oz/2 cups caster sugar and 150ml/¼ pint/⅔ cup water. Allow it to rest in the refrigerator for 12 hours.
3   Wearing latex gloves, colour half the fondant pink. If you like, you could leave all the fondant white. (You could also make it brown or grey.)
4   Shape the fondant into 6 pear shapes with flat bottoms; 3 white and 3 pink. Carefully mould the ears, using a sugar shaping tool or a wooden skewer, to form indentations the coffee beans can sit in snugly.
5   Push the coffee beans into the shaped ears, then add silver balls or other decorations for eyes. (You could add a ball for a nose, if you like.)
6   Cut lengths of string for the tails. Using sugar working tools or a wooden skewer, push them into place.
7   Allow the mice to dry completely overnight at room temperature.

Energy 1164kcal/4956kJ; Protein 5.4g; Carbohydrate 271.8g, of which sugars 43.2g; Fat 2.3g, of which saturates 1.4g; Cholesterol 0mg; Calcium 31mg; Fibre 0.1g; Sodium 18mg

Index

acid drops 26
anise, star: honey and star anise
   chews 52
aniseed twists 34

barley sugar sticks 36
boiled sweets
   acid drops 26
   aniseed twists 34
   bull's eyes 30
   candy canes 38
   lemon drops 22
   pear drops 24
   peppermint humbugs 32
   rhubarb and custards 28
bull's eyes 30

candy canes 38
chews
   honey and star anise chews 52
   maple cream candy 54
   pineapple chews 56
Christmas: candy canes 38
cream: maple cream candy 54
cream dreams, lemon 60
custards, rhubarb and 28

dip, sherbet 46
dried fruits: jewelled lollipops 44

Edinburgh rock, rose water 40

fondant
   fondant-stuffed pecans 58
   lemon cream dreams 60
   sugar mice 62
   working with 16–17
fruit sherbet 46

hard candy
   acid drops 26
   aniseed twists 34
   bull's eyes 30
   candy canes 38
   lemon drops 22
   pear drops 24
   peppermint humbugs 32
   rhubarb and custards 28
honey and star anise chews 52
humbugs, peppermint 32

jewelled lollipops 44

lemon
   barley sugar sticks 36
   lemon cream dreams 60
lemon drops 22
lollipops
   jewelled lollipops 44
   raspberry lollipops 42

maple cream candy 54

nuts
   fondant-stuffed pecans 58

jewelled lollipops 44
lemon cream dreams 60
maple cream candy 54

orange: fondant-stuffed pecans 58

pear drops 24
pecans, fondant-stuffed 58
peppermint: candy canes 38
peppermint humbugs 32
pineapple chews 56
pistachio nuts: jewelled lollipops 44

raspberry lollipops 42
rhubarb and custards 28
rock, rose water Edinburgh 40
rose water Edinburgh rock 40
rum: pineapple chews 56

salt-water taffy 50
sesame seeds: honey and star anise
   chews 52
sherbet
   fruit 46
   lemon 22
sour drops 26
star anise: honey and star anise
   chews 52
sugar mice 62
sugar syrup, making a 12–13

taffy
   salt-water taffy 50
   working with 18–19
testing for a set 14–15
twists, aniseed 34

walnuts: maple cream candy 54